Please return items on or before the Due Date printed on your receipt.
Register your email address and you will receive a reminder before your books are due back.
You can register your email address, check the Due Date and renew your loans online at
www.dublincitypubliclibraries.ie
Have your Library Card Number and PIN to hand.
You can also renew your loans in person or by phone.

Leabharlanna Poiblí Chathair Bhaile Átha Cliath
Dublin City Public Libraries

Comhairle Cathrach
Bhaile Átha Cliath
Dublin City Council

D1333638

Your Dublin Travel Guide
Seeing Dublin on a Budget

Copyright © 2019 N. T. Gore

Table of Contents

Irish phrase "sure, there's a grand stretch in the evenings".

During the fall and the winter weather is mild for the most part except for the random bouts of below freezing temperatures with scarce amounts of snowfall, if any. The average temperature during the fall is between 57 degrees Fahrenheit and 64 degrees Fahrenheit. The coldest months are typically January and February with 46 degrees Fahrenheit temperatures, if not a little bit warmer or colder.

You might be asking yourself "When is the best time to visit Ireland?" Well, the answer is simple – there isn't a "best time" to visit, it is entirely based upon your personal preference!

Want to visit during peak vacationer time? Then pick a summer month like July or August when Ireland is at its peak visitor season. Vacationing during the summer will give you the opportunity to see parks in full bloom during the day or during the sunny evenings. You may enjoy dining al fresco at the cafes or visiting the many festivals!

Would you rather visit during a less packed time of the year? Well, then you're going to want to go sometime in the fall or

spring. During the fall you can kick about the multi-colored leaves or pile them up and laugh as you dive into them, rinse and repeat! Ireland is beautiful during this time of year, so it also opens up for many photo shoots! If you plan to go during the winter you should take a nice crisp walk through the national park.

If you are wondering about how to pack for the weather, you should be adaptable. Long sleeves, short sleeves, pants, shorts – the whole nine yards! Bring a hoodie for the chilly days and quite possibly bring a waterproof jacket for the random down pour! Definitely bring comfortable walking shoes if you plan on doing a lot of day trips!

When is it Warm?

January's average maximum temperature is forty-eight degrees Fahrenheit, whilst July's average maximum temperature is sixty-eight degrees Fahrenheit. As you can see, the difference between winter and summer temperatures is not very large. Nice and mild for a vacation spot, don't you think? Layered clothing will work year-round. Just don't

forget to bring an umbrella and a bottle of sun block, just in case.

Getting Around Dublin

The thought of traveling in a city you are unfamiliar with can be intimidating, but when you add in the different country factor to the equation it can often be off-putting. Luckily, like most of the world, travelers will find that public transport is very similar. Which makes it relatively easy to find your way around a new environment, and how to do it as cheaply as possible.

There are six basic modes of transportation in Dublin, Ireland. The Dart, buses, the Luas, taxis, by foot, and by rental car! Below you will find a compilation of the six ways to travel in Dublin, hopefully it will make your travel needs easier!

The Dart:

An acronym for Dublin Area Rapid Train, a fast and frequently used mode of transportation in Dublin City by locals

and tourists alike. The train hugs the Irish Sea coast for most of the scenic journey, making it one of the most beautiful ways to travel.

The electric rail system follows the eastern coastline from Malahide and/or Howth in North Dublin. It continues right through the city centre to the southern suburbs such as Blackrock, and then it continues onto the coastal towns such as Bray and Greystones.

Dublin is a popular place for travelers to arrive and depart from while they are exploring the rest of Ireland, by rail mostly. A traveler's favorite mode of transportation because of the beautiful scenery along the coastline, it's complete heaven!

Buses:

We've all seen a European bus before, on movies such as Harry Potter, or online in some form or another, so it shouldn't be too difficult to picture it. Either single or double Decker buses,

most of which start their days on or near O'Connell street, Abbey street, and Eden quay on the north side. If you are on the south side buses typically start on or near Aston Quay, College street, and Fleet street. However, you can typically find a handful of bus stops on each street in Dublin.

Look for the big blue or green lollipop signs around the city, but make sure you know where that bus is going next! You can find this out by looking at the destination street and bus number posted above the front window. The buses headed for the city centre will have a weird looking label written in a cross between Latin and Gaelic – VIA AN LAR.

On Monday through Saturday from 6am to 11pm you can catch a bus, on Sundays the buses run from 10am to 11:30pm. However, the Nitelink – a bus specifically running on Fridays and Saturdays – you can catch this bus anywhere from midnight to 4am.

Buses typically run on thirty-minute

increments, you can find a bus schedule posted at the revolving notice boards at any bus stop around Dublin if you want a more set time frame for the day.

The fare for the buses is relatively well-priced. Inner-city fares are distance based, however during the day there is a designated "city centre zone" which will cost € 0.70. However, this zone only covers from Parnell Square in the north to Connolly Station and Merrion Square in the east, St. Stephen's Green in the south and Ormond Quay in the west. Longer journeys will cost between €1.75 and €5.

When you are ready to pay you will do so on-board using the automatic fare machine in the front of the bus. Forms of payment include coins or a smart card known as a Leap Card. A Leap Card is HIGHLY RECOMMENDED especially if you intend to use the buses to get around during your entire stay in Dublin. It should be noted that most buses will not make change; you will be handed a change receipt that you will take to the

Dublin Bus Headquarters on O'Connell street to receive your change.

The Airlink – route 747 – which runs between the Airport and the city centre will be your best bet if you want to make change without a hassle. Those bus drivers are more likely to make the change for you; however, you should always be prepared for the possibility that you will not be given change.

The Luas:

"Luas" is the Gaelic word for speed, so this mode of transportation is aptly named as it is Dublin's light-rail transit. It is a swift and reliable way to travel, the tram crosses the city on two lines to get people where they need to be quickly and efficiently.

Your ticket will be purchased at a street side vending machine and can be bought for a single trip, returning trip, or you can purchase a flexi-ticket which will cover your travels for either seven days or a full thirty days.

There are two separate lines that the Luas travels on; the Red and the Green. Make sure you research and get on the correct line for your traveling wishes.

The Luas Red Line – a thirty-two stop trip – runs from Tallaght in the west through the city centre to Point Village or Saggart/Connolly Station.

The Luas Green Line – a twenty-two stop trip – runs from St. Stephen's Green through Ranelagh and Dundrum to Brides' Glen in the south.

During the journey on the Luas Red you will encounter several points of interest such as the 3 Arena, the National Museum of Decorative Arts & History at Collins Barracks as well as Kilmainham Goal.

During the journey on the Luas Green you will encounter points of interest such as the foodie village of Ranelagh, the shopping area of Dundrum Town Centre, and many other beautiful sights along the way.

Taxi:

You probably wouldn't guess it by the way Ireland is portrayed, but Dublin is a very common place to find Taxis. They are a cheap way to travel, and it gives you the opportunity to talk to a local who knows a thing or two about Dublin – and maybe some hidden gems that you wouldn't find in a travel guide or online.

You can catch a taxi in a number of ways such as hailing one from the street, calling for one on the phone, or you will find them at populated areas like the hotels and bus stations/train stations.

Leap Cards!

As previously mentioned, a Leap Card is a must if you plan on traveling around the city by bus multiple times daily. This card will provide you with a constant discount on public transport, which anybody could appreciate.

The card itself is a pre-paid smart card

for use on all Dublin Buses – Airlink and Nitelink included – DART, Luas, and commuter trains for a lower price. You have to pay for the refundable deposit, but the card is free. It is €5 for Adults, €3 for Children, and you must buy at least €5 worth of credit. However, it is well worth the initial price in the long run.

The card can be purchased at places where the distinctive green logo – depicting a seemingly over-excited frog is captured mid-leap – such as Easons at Dublin Airport, kiosks, and spa shops. You can also find them online at www.leapcard.ie or at the ticket machines in some city center DART and railway stations.

On Foot:

A large part of the world primarily travels by some form of public transport, or they drive themselves, however a fair amount of the population travels by foot. Not only is walking literally free, but is also keeps you healthy and active during the day – even though it sometimes isn't ideal to walk.

Luckily, for those who do prefer to travel by foot Dublin is a fairly compact city with some streets market as pedestrian only. But not all streets are, so make sure you look both ways before crossing the street on the zebra-stripes market street – most of which have a two blinking lights indicator.

Rental Car:

Don't prefer to travel by public transport? No problem! Just rent a car and drive yourself. However, it isn't necessarily suggested to do so inside of Dublin due to its compact size and European streets – very different than American streets.

If you are planning to travel around the rest of Ireland then you should absolutely rent a car!

Accommodations in Dublin

When you plan a vacation for yourself and your family/friends or even a solo trip, one of the first things that comes to mind is: Where am I going to sleep? And how can I make it the cheapest/best quality stay? That's where the next section of this guide comes in handy for someone like yourself.

Frequent vacationers will tell you that you need to book well in advance to your trip to avoid several issues such as overbooking hotels, overpriced stays, etc. and they are absolutely correct in their advice. Dublin is just like many other vacation spots, hotels go fast and then what is left gets jacked up to add money to the hotel's pocket. Especially during the peek vacation times of the year.

From June to August – similar to North America's hotel pattern – it is incredibly hard to find a hotel within your price range, and sometimes it is hard to find one at all! So, book early to avoid these problems. It is suggested to book at least two months in advance to give you the best price range and the best hotel location for your vacationing needs.

If you are less interested in visiting during the summer you can book from November to February during their down season, although Christmas can get a little hectic.

It is advised to be wary of cheaper, farther away hotels as the quality of the hotels can sometimes not match up to the price you pay, as with any vacation spot. Even if you are willing to travel a little farther for a cheaper price, you may want to make sure you research all your options before booking the hotel.

Below you will find a compiled list of some of the best hotels as picked by us in three categories: Cheaper, Closest, and Lavish. However, if you do not find a hotel you like from this list, you can always do more extensive research on websites like Kayak.com or Hotels.com.

Beds on a Budget

Holiday Inn Express Dublin – Airport.
Located less than ten minutes from the airport and six-hundred and fifty feet from the Crowne Plaza's Conference Center, this hotel is cheap and comfortable with air-conditioned rooms and a free shuttle to and from the airport.

The room has many amenities worth its price range such as the interactive TVs, free wired internet, work desks for the traveling business person, hair dryers, irons and coffee makers/tea making stations. There is also a continental breakfast, included in the hotel price, and the lounge has a fully licensed bar with live sports playing on the TVs.

Location-wise it is less than three miles from the National Show Center and National Botanic Gardens. Plus, the bonus of transportation to the city's center and Croke Park!

Glashaus Hotel.

With spacious rooms, cozy beds and a fully stocked bar in the lounge this hotel offers comfort for a cheap price tag! Twenty-four-hour room service, LCD TVs and free Wi-Fi are also included in the hotel's amenities

The location is just fifteen minutes away from the War Memorial Gardens and Tallaght Stadium.

The Metro Hotel Dublin Airport.

Our last 'cheap' option is also in a great location, with Dublin City University, the

National Botanic Gardens and Croke Park just minutes away!

Inside of the hotel you will find several places to relax such as a restaurant, a bar/lounge, and a Cafe. However, due to the number of places to receive food within its vicinity, room service is only available during a set number of hours per day.

Amenities include Wi-Fi, an airport shuttle with a surcharge available on request, guest parking with a fee, concierge services and dry cleaning/laundry facilities. There are also complimentary newspapers in the lobby if you want to get a taste of Irish news, guestrooms available, and direct dial telephones with voicemail.

If you so choose to get a guestroom its amenities include, DVD players, coffee makers/tea making stations, laptop-compatible safes, digital TV and a hairy dryer.

Hotels with the Best Locations

Holiday Inn Express Dublin City Centre.

While the price for a room at this hotel is higher than the previously listed hotels, the location benefit pays for the difference. The hotel is only a fifteen-minute drive on the M50 motorway for a quick link to the rest of the country, while intercity transport is also available to you from the Heuston train station and a quick connection to the Dublin airport.

Tram and bus stops litter the streets for easy access to the rest of the city, with the benefit of a twenty-four-hour car park to keep your rental car secure during the night while you sleep, and during the day if you choose to leave it while you explore the city!

You also have the option of walking as well, with Grafton Street close by for some amazing shopping and the popular night life district where you will find the frequented Temple Bar. If shopping and drinking isn't on your to-do list don't fret!

You can also watch some amazing concerts at the 3Arena, or you can go watch a game of international Rugby at the Aviva Stadium! A taxi can get you there in fifteen minutes, maybe less depending on traffic! A twenty-minute walk can get you to the National Gallery of Ireland across the River Liffey, where you can gaze at spectacular painting by Picasso and Rembrandt.

The hotel itself offers many amazing amenities such as free Wi-Fi, Express Star Breakfast, a Cafe and Bar, and three air-conditioned conference rooms for business meetings – with the possibility of catering for the longer meeting days.

Arlington Hotel O'Connell Bridge. Another hotel in a marvelous location! Just 0.3 miles (or .48 kilometers) from the Spire, Abbey Theater, Temple Bar, and Trinity College. A short fifteen-minute walk gets you to Dublin Castle, St. Stephen's Green, and the Natural History Museum – also in walking distance of many restaurants and nightclubs.

However, the hotel offers two restaurants of its own if you would rather eat at the hotel before you go out sight-seeing or before you retire upstairs for bed.

Other hotel amenities include free Wi-Fi, guestrooms, and amazing bathrooms with a makeup mirror, shower/tub combination, complimentary soaps, hair dryer and on request you will receive an iron/ironing board, and a crib if you are traveling with an infant.

The guestroom's amenities include, desks, TVs, direct dial phones, coffee makers/tea making stations, and a trouser press.

Academy Plaza Hotel.

The final best location hotel to be mentioned is the Academy Plaza hotel, a family owned business with nineteen years of exceptional guest services. It is located ideally, just off of O'Connell street near the Pear, with Temple Bar, Croke Park Stadium, the business district and Dublin convention centre and Rotunda Hospital just a short distance away!

It is also easy to get to with the Airlink stopping in front of the hotel as well as the well-connected city transportation network – buses, the local tram Luas, and the Dart rail.

The hotel has over three hundred rooms with your choice of single, double, twin or triple, quadruple, executive and wheelchair accessible rooms. The rooms have been remodeled recently making them fresh and new-feeling!

Other amenities include free Wi-Fi, flat screen TVs, phones, laptop-compatible safes, double glazed windows, air-conditioning, iron and ironing boards, showers or bathtubs, a hair dryer, and a work desk.

Complimentary tea or coffee is offered to you, to ensure that your stay is as lovely as possible. On the ground floor you have access to a gym between the hours of 6am to 11pm, with computers in the lobby for guests to use.

Larger business events can be held in three different sized conference rooms, the largest can hold up to one-hundred and twenty people. Each room holds an LCD projector with a projector screen, whiteboard, flip-chart, pads and pens, and stationery with refreshments. Upon request you can hire additional catering.

Parking is available in the car park across the street from the hotel, for a discounted rate if you stay at the hotel. Luggage assistance is also available to you, twenty-four hours a day, and storage can be arranged after check out for up to eight hours. However, early check in is available and it may affect your luggage storage.

Lavish Hotels...

The Westbury Hotel.
Located in the city center just off of Grafton street, The Westbury Hotel is located very ideally. Enjoy the main shopping district, and journey to Trinity College or to Stephen's Green for a little historic journey. Shopping, drinking and

dining is within grasp due to the hotel's location, but that's not all, enjoy some of the best night life and theaters Dublin has to offer!

Hotel amenities include free Wi-Fi, free newspaper in the lobby, laundry facilities, luggage storage, free infant beds, tour/ticket assistance, fireplace in the lobby, and much more to enjoy during your stay at the Westbury hotel.

The hotel room amenities include premium TV channels, hypo-allergenic bedding available on request, premium default bedding, soundproof rooms, air-conditioning, blackout curtains, mini bar, free toiletries, twenty-four-hour room services and bathrobes.

These are just a few of the amenities available in your hotel room, there is much more to enjoy about the Westbury! Like, flat-panel TV and espresso machine for example.

Inside of the hotel you an dine at Cafe Novo or the restaurant Wilde. Not to mention the fitness room, the use of a computer near the business center with complimentary internet.

If you are a business person you would be interested in hearing that the hotel has a conference room with seen bedrooms, and the Grafton suite which holds up to two-hundred and twenty people. The room also has its own entrance.

The Merrion Hotel.

The final hotel is a five-star hotel located on Merrion Street Upper near Stephen's Green, just a short walk away from shopping on Grafton street. A short walk can also get you to the National Museum of Ireland!

If walking sounds like a strenuous task, don't fret! Once you have finished your day of sight-seeing you can return to the hotel and enjoy the day spa inside the hotel! Treat yourself to some pampering because you're worth it.

A day spa isn't the only thing this hotel has, it also has two restaurants – one of which, Restaurant Patrick Guilbaud, has received two Michelin stars! After some great food you can enjoy a drink at the hotel bar/lounge, a nice Irish whiskey or a pint.

Other hotel amenities include an indoor pool, a sauna, a fitness center, free Wi-Fi, luggage storage, rooftop terrace, dry-cleaning/laundry facilities, wedding services, bellhops and staff members that speak multiple languages!

Room amenities include air-conditioning, free bottled water, free newspapers, bidets, LCD TVs, premium bedding, mini bar, hair dryer, separate bath tub and shower, satellite TV, desks, hypo-allergenic bedding available on request and twenty-four-hour room service!

Restaurants & Food

Everyone loves to eat. It's just a universal truth no matter where you're from, what race, sex, or religion you are. People love to eat.

Well, Ireland just happens to be one of those places where the food is just as good as the drink is. You've heard that Ireland is the home of the potato, presumably. Well, there is truth in that, a decent amount of meals in Ireland do consist of potatoes in some form, shape, or fashion.

Below you will find a list of the best restaurants to eat at during your stay in the beautiful, lush country of Ireland.

Accompanied by a list of prices, ranging from less than expensive, moderately expensive, all the way to the more expensive priced places. Of course, these prices are subject to changes due to size of party, whether or not you order alcoholic beverages, desert etc.

Even though it may jump your bill a little, you should definitely try some of the deserts and drinks because, why not? You're on vacation! Allow yourself to enjoy the culture and all that comes with it!

Dublin's Top 15 Restaurants

Average price per person

$ = Less than € 20 (Less than $22 USD)

$$ = €20 - €40 ($22 - $45 USD)

$$$ = €40 – €60 ($45 - $68 USD)

$$$$ = More than €60 (More than $68 USD)

1   L Mulhgan Grocer ($$)

- 20th – century Dublin pub, remodeled as a great food environment.

- The menus come tucked into books. (Primarily popular children's books).

- The bill comes with a bag of candy. Despite its playfulness, the cooking is quite sophisticated with brilliant Irish ingredients, such as

Gubbean Chorizo, and grass-fed free-range meat.

- Farmhouse cheeses to be paired very well with cigars, gins, whiskeys, and craft beers.

2   Oxmantown ($)

- 'Ox' comes from the Viking word for "eat".

- To this small establishment the art of sandwich making is taken very seriously. One example is the Breakfast sandwich with an added side of Jack McCarthy's Black Pudding.

3   Fish Shop ($$)

- Husband-and-wife team Peter Hogan and Jumoke Akintola met in London as trainee teachers, they set up a street-food stall as a hobby. Eventually they decided to quit teaching, returned to Dublin, and opened a fish shack.

- Two years later they opened this very Queen street restaurant and then a second chip shop and wine bar. Only serves Wild Irish fish.

- The menu changes depending on the catch at sea, however the short but inspired wine list is served by the glass.

4   Da Mimmo ($$)

- Originally opened as a small pizza/pasta place. Family-run neighborhood restaurant. Healthy takeaway pizza trade.

- Small, rustic Italian cooking in a tiny dinning room. Serves Spaghetti and clams, woodsy risotto with Italian sausage – liberal amounts of cream butter and parmesan.

5 Chapter One ($$$$)

- Michelin-starred restaurant in the basement of the Dublin Writer's Museum.

- Special occasion restaurant and Chef Ross Lewis uses the best ingredients.

- Food combinations like wild turbot with cucumber gazpacho, langoustine dumplings, and white asparagus.

- Specialty dishes such as Sika venison with salted baked parsnip or wood-pigeon tarine.

- Important to note that

Friday and Saturday night tables are booked well in advance, and it is easier to get Lunch and theatre seats.

6   Mr. Fox ($$$$)

- Fairly new.

- Chef Anthony Smith creates delicious dishes. During Winter and Spring try the Deer Tartare!

- Playful deserts inspired by sweet shops and ice-pop flavors.

7   Terra Madre ($$)

- Itsy-bitsy basement restaurant down an old stone staircase. Great 'Irish peasant' cuisine. Featuring dishes like Tuscan stews – octopus and black chickpeas.

- Italian-esque cooking as well – lardo served

warmly over toast with imported Italian fennel salami with a side of pickled caper sprouts.

8   Rosa Madre ($$)

- Quiet, friendly atmosphere, nice owner Luca de Marzio. Try anything that Luca recommends, because there is no denying that it will be good.

- Worthy mentions from the menu include Dublin Bay prawns, scallops diced in shell with breadcrumbs and parmesan.

9   Piglet ($$)

- A wine bar with big flavor goals. Brainchild of owner/wine importer Enrico Fantasia.

- Serves dishes such as

smoked eel topped with
bean puree and goat
bacon on toasted
sourdough.

- Like Italy and Ireland had
  a baby, and their food
  was delicious!

10 Chameleon ($$)

- One of the oldest spots in
  Temple Bar! On a quiet
  road in the direction of
  River Liffey.

- Indonesian food. Offers a
  set menu feast or the
  option of a series of small
  plates.

- A specialty worth
  mentioning is the house
  beef short rib, cooked for
  at least ten hours, with a
  sweet blackened star
  anise crust.

- Vegetarians will also find
  something delicious here

with the Balinese Curry. A creamy coconut, butternut squash and string bean meal.

11 Klaw ($$)

- Itsy-bitsy crab shack. Oysters, raw or blow-torched in their shell, are brought to your table for standing for so long.

- Best place in town for your first taste of native Irish oysters.

- A strangely delicious meal is the crab BLT.

12 The Pepper Pot Café ($)

- A quaint place with balcony seating and a typical wild line on the weekends.

- The best bagels in Dublin. Cooked that day for the freshest quality bagels.

- The weird combination of

pear and bacon will entice you as you enjoy the Pear and Bacon sandwich.

- Fresh, crumbly scones held together by a dollop of clotted cream and house-made raspberry jam.

13 The Greenhouse ($$$$)

- Michelin-starred food cooked by Chef Mickael Viljanen.

- Chef Viljanen is adventurous with his food, and with his masterful skills everything he cooks is guaranteed to be delicious. Like the Celeriac with a rye skin – delightful to eat.

14 Hatch & Sons Irish Kitchen ($$)

- In the basement of The

Little Museum of Dublin.

- Chef Domini Kemp is one of the brilliant minds behind some of the restaurant's best meals, such as Guinness stew with platters of cheese, fish, and bread.

- Primarily Breakfast and Lunch, however the restaurant stays open until 9 pm on Wednesdays and Thursdays.

15 Taste at Rustic ($$$)

- Dylan McGrath built this out-of-the way attic restaurant above his other restaurant Rustic Stone. There are lots of stairs to climb, but the journey is well worth it.

- With Japanese techniques and Irish ingredients his dishes

are mind-blowingly
delicious.

Pubs and Bars

If you thought we weren't going to discuss Pubs, you were sorely mistaken! This next part is dedicated to the best pubs in Dublin – excluding the highly recognized and tourist-central Temple Bar.

19 Pubs to Drink at in Dublin

1.)The Brazen Head.

The oldest standing pub in Dublin and Ireland, dating all the way back to 1198. It is still as lively today as it was back then. Live music is played every night.

2.)O'Donoghue's.

Do not miss the opportunity to have a drink inside of this cozy pub, maybe after vising St. Stephen's Green? If you can manage to get inside of the packed pub, it is well worth the effort! You can hear some amazing traditional Irish music!

3.)The Long Hall.

This pub thankfully survived its reconstruction during the Celtic Tiger Boom! Drop in mid-week for a quiet pint, or if you are into the bustling pub scene visit during the weekend when it is jam-packed with people!

4.)McDaid's.

The first thing you may notice within this pub is the high ceilings, and if you're lucky you may just notice the trapdoor behind the bar leading down to the cellar! If you are settling in for an evening try going up the narrow staircase where you can enjoy a nice night of reading with a pint!

5.)L. Mulligan Grocer.

Do not order a Guinness or a Budweiser here! It is all crafts beer all the way! As the name suggests there was once a Grocer shop within the pub, but the rear of the pub is now a phenomenal restaurant serving Irish produce with a creative twist!

6.)Toner's.

A traditional pub that dates back all the way to 1818 with a wooden bar full of memorabilia and drawers that date back to the pub's older grocer days.

7.)The Cobblestone.

Drop in for some amazing traditional music and a pint here! Be prepared for a fair amount of noise with a foot tapping and thigh slapping good time!

8.)The Stag's Head.

Hidden away behind Dame Street, this pub is home to an ornate Victorian bar with lots of stained glass and wood finishing. There is a large stag's head that watches over the patrons as they enjoy an amazing night within its walls.

9.)Farrington's.

This pub, within the party-central part of Temple bar, has amazing craft beers and "tap takeovers" which is when a large selection of taps is dedicated to one brewery. You are definitely going to want to ask the bartender for a recommendation!

10.) Palace Bar.

Another pub at the edge of the Temple Bar area, where you may meet a great selection of close friends for life. With comfy chairs, witty conversations, and amazing drinks. People often stop in on their way to Temple Bar or come from Temple Bar to enjoy the cozy atmosphere.

11.) The Toast Bar.

Extremely modern and trendy bar with comfortable couches, low tables, and a student atmosphere. On the main road of Rathmines just one kilometer from Dublin City Centre. This bar is probably more centered towards students, but don't be afraid to pop on in for a pint or two!

12.) Rody Boland's.

On the same road as the Toast Bar, this

pub is another student-based pub – but it is also home to a lot of locals. The seemingly boring red door often fools people into thinking that it is just a small drinking place for a more senior crowd, but it is so much more than that! It is a deceivingly large pub that spans for about three city blocks on the inside, and normally is chalk full of people drinking and laughing.

13.) The Quays Bar.

Found in the tourist area of Temple Bar district, this friendly and traditional Irish pub is just a few pubs down from Oliver St. Gogarty's Pub. You will find traditional Irish music and traditional Irish dancing, lots of fun, friendly people and of course, a lot of Guinness! It is a tourist bar, but that doesn't make it any less of a fun place to drink and laugh the night away.

14.) Messrs. Maguire.

This pub is four stories high and overlooks the O'Connell Bridge and the River Liffey. Messrs. Maguire is a great place to sit and laugh with friends, or even a great place to make some friends! The building is from the 19th – century and can get a little confusing to navigate your way through the stairs, rooms and floors, so it is pretty ideal to know where you are planning to go. There is also a cafe inside, for those that may want a nice cappuccino instead of a frothy beer.

15.) Johnny Fox's Pub.

Not that well-known, but a truly magnificent and legendary pub! It is a more hush-hush bar that people only whisper about. This pub however, has a bit of a requirement – a car or cab fair. (Or a booze bus that runs there). The highest pub in Ireland, sitting atop the Dublin Mountains in Glencullen. A twenty-five-minute drive out of Dublin, but well worth the journey. Famous visitors such as the band U2 have been known to preform here!

16.) The Porterhouse.

This pub is known to be one of THE best

for live music! Traditional, acoustic, bands, you name it! It sits just at the edge of Temple Bar district so it does attract a fair number of tourists! The pub is also a favorite of Dubliners. There are four floors to drink on, dance on, laugh on, and generally have a great time with balconies for you to view the live music going on below. There are beers brewed in house as well! A great place to take photos as there are giant copper vats within the pub!

17.) Cafe En Seine Bar.

A stylish bar on Dawson street, parallel to the shopping district known as Grafton street! So, if you have had an amazing, drop-dead day of shopping and are feeling an equally amazing night of drinking this is definitely a place to hit up. It is a blend of 19th – century Persian décor with Irish style beer! The crowd is young professional meets older and tourist. You can buy tickets to the killers New Year's Eve night!

18.) McSorley's Pub.

Local, student area pub in Ranalegh village. Catch live sports, and have an amazing time drinking some Kilkenny with your pals! The locals may even join in on your fun evening as they enjoy the live sports and quite possibly explain them to you.

19.) Zanzibar.

As the name suggests this is a very unique and wondrous place to drink. North of the River Liffey, Zanzibar's décor is something out of a movie with its plush velvety cushions, humongous urns, palm trees, Eastern paintings and a spacious two stories for a great evening to be had! You are going to want to arrive early if you want to beat the packed times, as this bar is VERY popular and busy most nights and often has a line to get in. The beer can be a little pricey, so this bar is a little more about the company and the décor than the actual drinking. Definitely worth a visit!

Just as with the restaurants here, there

are many other pubs and bars within Dublin and Ireland entirely. It would take way too long to list them all, and that is another book entirely. These are just some of the more notable bars and pubs in the area.

We intentionally did not include The Temple Bar in this list as it is the most popular tourist area pub and deserved a list all its own – a honorable mention if you will – as follows on the next pages. So let's move on.

Dublin's Best Sights

The Temple Bar

This street in central Dublin named "Temple Bar" is by far the most visited by tourists. There is not even a little bit of competition in numbers. The street is lined with boutiques, cafes, shopping, and pubs. You can plan an entire day in this area of Dublin alone! It is jam-packed with tourists going about their day and partying their nights away in the bars and pubs that line the streets here.

Don't misunderstand, there is in fact a pub called Temple Bar, with its red exterior and excellent live music. Many tourists and locals alike do tend to enjoy their nights within its historical walls. There is a heated beer garden for you to enjoy a quiet, cozy meal and a pint. With the largest selection of whiskey in Ireland how could you go wrong?

The bar has at least three musical sessions daily from 2pm until close, seven days a week. Temple Bar won the award for "Irish Music Pub of The Year" every year from 2003 until 2013, So you can expect to have an amazing time enjoying the best music!

Feel free to bar hop to one of the many other bars in the Temple Bar district. Such as The Auld Dubliner, Foggy Dew, Oliver St. John Gorgarty's Hostel, The Norsemen, The Palace Bar, and many, many others! With so many choices to choose from you are sure to have an amazing time out with friends, family, or even solo enjoying the culture and the locals.

Hopefully this offered you enough information to have a killer night – or a couple of nights – out drinking from dusk till dawn with some of the coolest people in Dublin! Be sure to enjoy some of the food while you are visiting the Temple Bar district, as well. Not only to avoid getting sick, but also because the Irish cuisine is truly to die for!

Popular things to do in Dublin

The (Actual) Temple Bar.

•Famous because of its red exterior, and being one of the best nightlife scenes in Dublin. Great location in the center of Dublin. Most frequented bar by tourists and locals alike.

The Church.

•Beautiful and unique building. A restored Cathedral turned bar. Its name is a play on words from the old building's "St. Mary's Church" closed in 1964 and reopened in 2007 as a bar/nightclub.

•The main floor is the bar, with a gorgeous island bar/bar stools, booths and a small stage where from 7pm to 9pm you can expect to hear Irish music playing on Sunday through Wednesday.

•The downstairs is where the night life comes alive, with a DJ who plays all popular music and R&B tracks from 10pm to 3am on Fridays and Saturdays.

Guinness Storehouse Factory.

● One of the most popular tourist attractions in Dublin. Designed to look just like a pint of Guinness from the inside. (Known to be the largest pint in the world.)

● A ticket to the factory costs roughly €18.

● The tour consists of seven floors, where you will learn of Irish brewing history, the Guinness family, and how the stout beer is crafted. At the end of the tour you will be dropped off at the Gravity Bar.

Tour the Old Jameson Distillery.

● Used to be the original crafting place for Jameson whiskey. Production halted in the early 1970s. A tour takes you through the history and creation of Jameson whiskey, with the opportunity to taste the whiskey. If you haven't already then you will enjoy the first taste where it all began, and if you have then you will appreciate the history lesson of one of your favorite whiskeys.

●You will also be given an exclusive "Whiskey Taster Certificate" to prove your knowledge of its history.

Take a photo with The Spire of Dublin.

●The Spire of Dublin proudly stands approximately one-hundred and twenty meters above ground, completely stainless-steel. About three meters in diameter at the base and fifteen centimeters at its apex.

●Picture it beautifully illuminated by the sunshine during the day, and at night the very tippy top of the structure is artificially lit up to look like a beacon into the sky.

St. Patrick's Cathedral.

●The largest church in Ireland, one of two built on Dublin soil, however it is the more popular tourist attraction of the two.

● Originally founded in 111, over 800 years of Irish history and culture within its walls. It is the final resting place of Author and former Dean, Jonathan Swift, who wrote Gulliver's Travels and A Modest Proposal.

Dublin Castle.

● A prehistoric tour of Dublin Castle, either by yourself or choose to get a guided-tour.

● Enjoy over 800 years of Irish memorabilia, from the grounds to the many rooms, gardens, and museums. Some rooms worth mentioning are the Chapel Royal, the Chester Beatty Library, the Garda Museum, and the Revenue Museum.

Ha'Penny Bridge.

● This bridge was the first pedestrian bridge built to span over the River Liffey in 1816. Its name comes from the price people used to pay to cross, a halfpenny.

- Today the bridge is one of Dublin's many tourist attractions. Seen on postcards, tourist brochures, and book covers.

Visit Christ Church Cathedral.

- Visit Dublin's second medieval Cathedral. Known also as The Cathedral of the Holy Trinity. Fully operational Roman Catholic church, considered to be the Cathedral of the United Dioceses of Dublin and Glendalough.

- Because the state does not fund the church, tourists are charged a modest fee to get in, however the fee is well worth it to see the beautiful history within its walls.

Picnic in Phoenix Park.

- 1,700 acres of walled in park just two miles from downtown Dublin. Also, home to Dublin Zoo, a sports field, the Wellington Monument, and both presidential and US Ambassador's

Residences.

Trinity College Library.

●A bibliophile's dream heaven! Largest library in all of Ireland and a beautiful piece of architecture.

●Home to the famous Book of Kells, an ornate and beautifully-crafted piece of literature. Between its pages you will find all four Gospels of the New Testament, over one-thousand-years old.

●The Long Room has been compared to the Jedi Archives from Star Wars. The main Library is only open to staff, graduates, and students. However, tourists are allowed to view the old Library within its quarters.

Lunch at Avoca Wool Shop & Cafe.

●When you think of Ireland one of two things comes to mind "booze and greenland". But Ireland is also known for its wool and mohair products. This small shop, named Avoca is known to sell wool products from the wool mill in the small town outside of Dublin Avoca.

●After you have browsed and hopefully bought a lovely piece from the shop you can travel upstairs to the Cafe for some lunch or maybe a coffee.

Tour Kilmainhan Gaol.

●An abandoned prison with a sad and spooky history. The restored building offers tourists a chance to take a guided-tour of the halls.

●A cheap ticket costs €4 per person, and you get a 45-50-minute tour of the prison's halls.

●The tour takes you on a journey to tell the tale of extreme prisoner treatment and countless other political knowledge you wouldn't get without taking it. With the benefit of learning of the restoration of the building.

Wicklow Mountains

●Tour Wicklow Mountains during the

day, known to be the filming location for the movie P.S. I Love You.

● Enjoy a nice day out with a guided-tour of the area. Don't forget your camera for some beautiful landscapes and maybe a selfie or two!

The Dublin Zoo.

● Journey to Phoenix Park where you will find the Dublin Zoo, and with the convenience of location you could return to the park later for a nice picnic or even just a nice jog.

● At the Zoo you will find a huge selection of animals to look at, all of which are very well looked after! Other cool benefits are a well-laid out map and a Cafe called Meerkat Cafe where you can get a coffee or a pastry while you watch the Meerkats playing.

The Dublin Flea Market.

● Huge indoor flea market on the last Sunday of every month.

- With over sixty stalls selling reusable household items you are sure to leave here with several exciting things! And quite possibly a few things you may not 'need'. Shh, it's okay we all do it!

The Glasnevin Cemetery Museum.

- Wander – respectfully! – through some of the graveyards where famous Irish politicians, poets, authors and more have been laid to rest.

- You will be given commentary on each person in the graveyards. Tickets cost anywhere from €6 to €25.

St. Stephen's Green.

- Another lush park to enjoy in Dublin.

- Lots of activities for groups as well as solo. Walking, jogging, biking, reading, picnicking, or relaxing on a nice day.

Five Things to do as a Bonus

Experience Gaelic Games.

- Take traditional Irish recreational

gaming lessons, and just ten minutes away from Dublin City Center.

●Learn about games such as world-famous hurling and Gaelic Football – a combination of soccer, rugby, and basketball. A great group activity!

National Botanic Gardens.

●Who doesn't love nature, am I right? With lush gardens full of plants and flowers you will have a beautiful day here!

●Bring your camera and enjoy taking photos of all the greenery, the sculpture garden and the vegetable garden designed to look like an old castle! It is free to visit without a tour, and with a tour it is €5.

Little Museum of Dublin.

●Who doesn't love a good museum? Here you will find that most of the artifacts and trinkets are donated by the people of Dublin. Each piece has its own unique history behind it.

- You can find music, film, politics, history, literature and culture here. To get in you will pay €7.

National Museum of Ireland.

- A completely free museum! With worthy mentions such as the Viking exhibit, the gold artifact display and the collection of "bog men" which are bodies removed from the bogs around Ireland and preserved for your viewing pleasure. A completely free museum!

- With worthy mentions such as the Viking exhibit, the gold artifact display and the collection of "bog men" which are bodies removed from the bogs around Ireland and preserved for your viewing pleasure.

Irish Whiskey Museum.

- The whisky connoisseurs among us will be excited for this one! With a combination of whiskey and history you get a taste of Ireland's best qualities!

- Detailed history of all the different

types of whisky. At the end of the tour you will be given three different whiskeys to try, and if you purchase the VIP package you will be given a fourth to try.

Free Things to Do?

Trinity College.

- Wander around marveling at the beauty of this Ireland college. Where famous alumni such s Samuel Beckett, Bram Stoker and Jonathan Swift stood.

- Elegant courtyards for beautiful walks and photo shoots, neo-classical architecture, cricket grounds outside the Pavilion Bar.

Phoenix Park.

- A lovely and lush place to have a picnic, play music, take photos, read a good book from the library, you name it!

- Only one of many parks in the city!

Tour the President's House.

- This tour departs from phoenix park every Saturday on a first-come-first-serve basis.

Chester Beatty Library.

●Alfred Chester Beatty's collection of ancient books, scrolls, and other ancient works of literature came be found here!

Temple Bar's art collection.

●Features the local and international photographs worthy of the public's eye! Have a pint while you take in the beauty and sophistication.

North Bull Island.

●One of Ireland's most important national conservative areas. You can watch birds of at least one-hundred and eighty species and take the five-kilometer walk.

Celtic Gold.

●A National Museum with old Celtic and medieval treasures. Most famous works include the Tara Brooch and the Ardagh Chalice.

National Botanic Gardens.

●Lush gardens waiting to be

photographed, smelled and admired.

●The squirrels are also known to be playful and delightful to watch.

South Wall Walk.

●One-kilometer walks out to the Poolbeg lighthouse along the South wall.

Art Galleries.

●The National Gallery has a collection that spans across seven centuries, including a Caravaggio and striking portraits of Ireland. The Dublin City Gallery has mostly modern and contemporary art.

City Parks.

●Enjoy several local parks such as St. Stephen's Green (the busiest park), Croke Park, Phoenix Park, or Merrion Square Park. All of which are gorgeous and green.

Irish Museum of Modern Art.

●A former hospital turned into the country's foremost modern art gallery.

Science Gallery.

●Two-story gallery devoted to interactive exhibits that show how truly lovely and compelling science is. Spend the whole day nerding out with fellow science fans!

Henrietta Street.

●Lined with red-brick Georgian mansions from the 1700s, built for the truly wealthy Irishman of that time. Gorgeous architecturally and envious.

Fine Art and Vivid History, a branch of the National Museum located in the Collins Barracks building.

●Dates back to the early 18th – century. A mix of history, design and craftsmanship.

The Grand Canal.

●A truly grand journey from the leafy area of Portobello road towards the bustling Grand Canal Quay. Unofficially named 'silicon docks'.

National History at the 'Dead Zoo'.

●Dusty, weird, and Victorian. One of the oldest attractions in Dublin!

Podcast Tours.

●Donal Fallon (local historian) has created three short podcasts with the Fitzwilliam hotel. Great for the history buff who prefers to listen rather than read. Being a guest isn't a requirement to listen to the podcasts. Emerce yourself in this historical walk through time to the Easter Rising battles location and the City's Fashionista stops!

Dublin Bikes.

●40 locations with 450 bikes on demand. If you want to get the bike rental for free you need to rent it and return it in under 30 minutes.

Sandeman's New Dublin Tour.

•Free three-hour walking tour. Departs from Dame Street every day at 11am and 2pm. Sometimes there are more if it is in high demand.

Cheap-But-Great Day Trips

(Prices average USD65-75 per person and you can find current pricing on sites such as www.viator.com)

Wild Wicklow Tour including Glendalough from Dublin

• Trip from Dublin to the 'Garden of Ireland' Wicklow.

• A guided tour of the 6th – century monastic ruins of Glendalough.

• Breathtaking scenery and wild landscapes of Wicklow.

• A shopping stop at Avoca Handweavers.

• Sally's Gap offers the chance to view where some of the movie Brave Heart was filmed.

• For lunch, visit an Irish Pub for some great Irish cooking and a pint.

- Dublin Bay at Sandycove.

- See the bridge where some of the movie P.S. I Love You was filmed.

Inclusions:

- Entrance fees.

- Professional guides.

- Complimentary whiskey tasting.

- Transportation is air-conditioned.

Exclusions:

- Hotel pick up and drop-off.

Additional:

- The minimum age for this tour is five years old, as the tour is not suited for infants.

- If there aren't enough passengers, the tour is subject to being canceled. If this happens you are given the option of an alternative tour, or a complete refund.

The general schedule:

- Meet your guide at one of the

designated pick up locations in central Dublin early in the morning. Journey through the exclusive suburbs of Sandycove and Dalkey before traveling through the rocky coastal backdrop of the Wicklow Mountains.

•Your first stop will be at Avoca Handweavers where you will be given the opportunity to do some shopping for some of Ireland's cultural handmade goods and other souvenirs. If you're feeling up to a nice cup of tea you can enjoy one before boarding your coach once more. However, it isn't included in the tour price so you will have to pay for it yourself.

•After shopping the journey continues onto the net leg where you will delve further into the Wicklow Mountains National Park and Sally Gap. You'll see the park's upper slopes, scenery that is blanketed in heath and bog. You will stop at Lough Tay "The Guinness Lake" where Brave Heart was filmed.

•By this point in your journey you will likely have built up an appetite. Enjoy lunch at a traditional Irish Pub, where you will find an Irish meal and a pint or a glass of Irish whiskey.

•Once your bellies are full and happy, your journey continues on to the last stop of the tour; The Monastic city of Glendalough. One of the most commonly visited cities in Ireland, named "Valley of the Two Lakes". It offers its visitors a peek into the rich cultural history of Ireland, and you will enjoy a guided tour of the many sites with time to explore solo.

•After re-boarding your coach, you will be given a free tot of Jameson whiskey while you wind down from the eight-and-a-half-hour journey. The coach will drop off its passengers at Dublin's Ballsbridge Hotel or Trinity College.

The Tour's Highlights:

- Full day trip from Dublin to Boyne Valley.

- Some of the oldest sites in Ireland with an expert guide.

- Six-thousand-year-old artwork carved into the passage tombs at Loughcrew.

- Stop in Louth country, where you will find the Celtic High cross of Mulredach in Monasterboice.

- Visit the Hill of Tara, where the High Kings once ruled over one-thousand years ago.

Inclusions:

- Educated local guide.

- Air-conditioned transport.

- A guided walking tour of Drogheda Town.

- A guided tour of Trim Castle. (The

entrance fee is included in the tour price; however, the keep is not.)

Exclusions:

●Lunch.

Additional:

●Children must be supervised at ALL times.

●The trip is subject to cancellation if there aren't enough passengers. You will be given the option of an alternative trip or a full refund.

General Schedule:

●Bright and early you will meet your guide/coach at Suffolk street. Your first destination will be Lough Crew Cairns, where you will follow the guide through beautiful stone passageways and marvel at the six-thousand-year-old petroglyphs.

●The next stop along your journey will be the ancient town of Trim, where you'll see Trim Castle set to the beautiful backdrop of River Boyne. You'll also be given the opportunity to go inside of the castle with a tour guide.

● Your journey will continue east to the Hill of Tara, where you will explore ancient monuments. The Hill of Tara is revered as the ceremonial seat of the Celtic High Kings from 1st -century AD through the 1100s. After you have explored the castle you will make your way back to Trim town for lunch, which is out of pocket.

● After a wonderful lunch the journey will continue north to the 18th – century Slane Castle on the way to Ardee. It is here where you will see the Jumping Wall, a 14th -century monument with a hilarious origin myth.

● Continuing your journey, you will come across Monasterboice, where you will see the gorgeous, and highly revered Celtic High cross of Muiredach – one of the most breathtaking pieces of Celtic stonework.

●The finale to your magical adventure happens to be a walking tour through ancient Drogheda. After your tour you will be given the opportunity to shop around the local shops before returning to the city – where you will be dropped off where you began on Suffolk Street.

Cliffs of Moher Tour including Wild Atlantic way and Galway City

The Tour's Highlights:

●Full day trip by coach from Dublin to the cliffs of Moher as well as the Burren and Galway city.

●Visit the Cliffs of Moher Visitor Experience, a state-of-the-art facility.

●Enjoy a casual walk through the cliffs, admire the views of Galway Bay and Aran Islands.

●Enjoy the Burren region, taking some photos along the way.

●Travel beside the scenic and wild Atlantic Way, a truly beautiful coastal route.

●Premium admission to the Visitor Centre is included and is a two hour stop.

●A two hour visit to Galway City comes with the opportunity to enjoy a complimentary guided walking tour of the city centre.

●You will be entertained by the driver's stories of Irish folklore, music, history, and lots of other fun!

Inclusions:

•Select hotel pickups.

•A professional tour guide.

•Entrance fee for the Cliffs of Moher is also included.

•*Guided walking tour of Galway City.*

Exclusion:

•Food and Drink.

•Gratuities (optional, but appreciated).

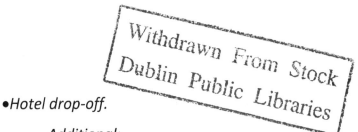
•Hotel drop-off.

Additional:

•Infant rates apply, provided they don't take up a seat.

•A moderate amount of walking is involved, so wear comfortable shoes.

•When purchasing your tickets, make sure to check the pickup locations in the special requirements field.

General Schedule:

•Early in the morning you will leave your hotel in an air-conditioned coach with free 4G Wi-Fi; specifically designed for the west coast of Ireland.

•As you travel, you will come across the truly gorgeous scenery that is Wild Atlantic Way, the Bunratty Castle, and the charming village of Lahinch on your journey to the Cliffs of Moher. You will also be given the opportunity to take a twenty-minute snack and coffee break.

•The café offers you the chance to

purchase food and drink before you get lost in the exhibits at the Cliffs of Moher Visitor Center. Enjoy the exhibits, like the Ledge – a virtual-reality cliff-face adventure – for a thrilling time! Don't forget to also capture some beautiful photos of the five mile (or eight kilometer) stretch of the Cliffs of Moher.

•Travel to Burren, where you will enjoy the lunar landscape with limestone quarries and plant species distinctive to the area.

•Head to Galway City, where you are given a thirty-minute walking tour of the city and harbor before exploring on your own.

•*You will return to your group at the given time and journey back to central Dublin, where your tour ends.*

Cliffs of Moher Day Trip from Dublin

The Tour's Highlights:

•A guided trip to the Cliffs of Moher.

- County Clare on Ireland's west coast.

- Unforgettable sights from the Cliffs of Moher, then over to the Aran Islands.

- Explore Doolin, a tiny town famous for its local music and four traditional Irish Pubs.

- An air-conditioned coach.

- Seventy-five minutes to explore the historic City of Galway.

- Bonus of entertaining guides and enthralling scenery.

Inclusions:

- Entrance to the Cliffs of Moher and Burren National Park.

- Air-conditioned coach with guide.

Exclusions:

- Lunch.

Additional:

- Infants welcome with their own, parent provided car seat.

General Schedule:

•Early in the morning you will depart from central Dublin, enjoying the commentary from your guide as well as the stunning Irish countryside.

•Journey along the pathways at the Cliffs of Moher, taking photos of the crashing waves against the Aran Islands, and gazing at the 702-foot (214 meter) summit.

•Next up you will enjoy lunch break in the village of Doolin, famous for beautiful local music. Listen to music and have a pint at one of the pubs.

•After lunch is over, journey to/through Burren National Park, catch a glimpse at the limestone region and search for rare exotic flowers.

•This concludes your tour, you will re-board the coach and journey back to central Dublin.

The Tour's Highlights:

•Ireland's top three attractions in a single day trip.

•Visit and kiss the famous Blarney Stone at Blarney Castle.

•Do some independent sightseeing in Cork City, your guide will offer some recommendations for you to see.

•A tour of the Rock of Cashel in County Tipperary.

•Transport is air-conditioned.

Inclusions:

•Entrance to Blarney Stone and the Rock of Cashel.

•Transport.

•Driver/guide.

Exclusions:

•Lunch.

Additional:

•Infants are welcome with their own parent provided car seat.

General Schedule:

•Arrive at Dublin central early in the morning where you will depart with your guide for the first destination. You will enjoy the commentary and the scenery on the journey.

•After going through truly gorgeous areas such as county Tipperary and county Kildare you will arrive at your first amazing stop; Castle Blarney. Here you will see the infamous, beloved Ireland treasure the Blarney Stone. You will travel up the castle's tower, where you will be encouraged to partake in the Irish tradition of kissing the Blarney Stone. According to legend, you will receive the skill of eloquent speech after you kiss the stone.

•Continue onto Cork City, you are given the opportunity to explore the city and relax for a while. At the English market you can purchase some lunch and then visit the triple-spired St. Finn Bar's Cathedral to gaze at the colossal structure.

•The final leg of the journey will bring you to the Rock of Cashel in county Tipperary, where you'll hear the legends of the Cathedral's twin towers and enjoy a guided tour of the halls of Vicars and Cormac's Chapel. (Home to the oldest Romanesque wall painting in Ireland.)

Giant's Causeway and Carrick-a-Rede Rope Bridge Day Trip from Dublin

Tour's Highlights:

•14-hour Giant's Causeway tour and Carrick-a-Rede Rope Bridge from Dublin.

•Visit both Giant's Causeway and the Carrick-a-Rede Rope Bridge in one Day Trip.

•Take photos of/at the Northern Ireland's Dunluce Castle.

•See one of Game of Throne's filming locations; the Dark Hedges.

•45 minutes in Belfast.

Inclusions:

•Free passage over the Carrick-a-Rede Rope Bridge when/if it's open.

•All other attractions are free as well.

•You will have a professional guide.

•Live on-board commentary about Ireland's magnificent history.

•Your transport is air-conditioned.

Exclusions:

•Food and Drink.

•Hotel pickups and drop-offs.

•Gratuities. (Are optional but appreciated.)

Additional:

•Small children or anyone with a severe difficulty with walking aren't recommended on this tour as there is a fair amount of walking. Make sure to wear comfortable shoes as well.

•It is also not recommended for anyone with a heart condition, back trouble, pregnant women, or other serious medical conditions.

•A group of twelve or more people, whether they are booked together or separately, they will not be accepted. The max seating is sixty people.

General Schedule:

•Early on in the morning you will meet your guide at central Dublin where you will begin the gorgeous journey to Belfast. You'll be there for forty-five minutes of wandering around and relaxing. Belfast is home to the famous feud between the Protestants and the Catholics.

•For fifteen minutes you will spend time at the filming location for Game of Thrones; Dark Hedges. You will also be given a photo opportunity at Dunluce

Castle for five minutes.

•Once the tour has come into Giant's Causeway, you'll have at least an hour and a half to gaze at the gorgeous seascape, and also have lunch here if you would like to do so.

•If you are brave enough to take the opportunity to cross the Carrick-a-Rede Rope Bridge! This Rope Bridge is sixty-five feet long (20 meters). The view is spectacular, and even if you don't cross the bridge you will still have an hour and a half to take some really amazing pictures.

•The journey will continue on to the beautiful towns of Bellycastle and Cushendum. You will catch glimpses of Sheep Island, Rathlin Island, and Scotland.

•The finale is twenty minutes in Cushendun before you will head back to Dublin.

Tour's Highlights:

•Day Trip from Dublin to Belfast, black cab tour and Giant's Causeway excursion.

•Game of Thrones filming location the
15 th – century Dunluce Castle.

•Belfast's top attractions such as Harland and Wolff Shipyard and Belfast Docks.

•Belfast's complex history will come alive at the Falls and Shankill neighborhoods. You will see hints of Ireland's complex history while cruising in a black cab.

•Travel along the Antrim coastal Drive while admiring the lush, beautiful scenery along the way.

•Giant's Causeway.

•Carrick-a-Rede Rope Bridge.

•Two hours stop at Giant's Causeway Visitor Centre. An optional complimentary walking tour of the Giant's Causeway Coast.

•Belfast Black cab Tour, a complete two-hour tour. Passengers will be able to walk and capture beautiful photos of various known troubled locations.

•Premium tickets to the Carrick-a-Rede Rope Bridge (optional to cross) where you'll spend an hour and a half.

Inclusions:

•Transport by a luxury coach with free Wi-Fi and air-conditioning.

•Entrance fees.

•Professional guide.

•Black cab transport in Belfast.

•Private guide.

•Entry to old Carrick-a-Rede Rope Bridge.

Exclusions:

•Food and Drink.

•Hotel pickup and drop-off.

Additional:

•Wear good walking shoes and all-weather clothing.

•Not wheelchair accessible.

•Check the pickup location at the checkout, in the special requirements section when buying the tickets.

General Schedule:

•Early in the morning meet your guide in central Dublin, with a twenty-minute coffee and snacks break before boarding the Black Cab tour in Belfast. You will also visit the same snack shop on the way back from your tour.

•You will explore Belfast's falls and Skankill neighborhoods, where you will learn about the city's industrial roots/divisive conflict. Compare that to its youthful revival in today's society.

•While you're enjoying the tour, some of Belfast's top attractions will draw your attention. Allow yourself to gaze upon gorgeous sites such as the Belfast Docks and the Harland and the Wolff Shipyard.

•Next up, you will come across the grand Antrim coastal Drive as you snap photos of the wild, rocky north coast and the hauntingly beautiful sea. You're going to want to catch a great look at the Dunluce Castle, snap a few photos to show your friends that you saw the shooting location for Game of Thrones House of Greyjoy!

•Back on the road again for two hours of driving until the tour reaches UNESCO World Heritage-listed Giant's Causeway. Here you will stretch your legs and wander around the gorgeous scenery for a while. Another great photo opportunity.

•The finale of this tour is a walk across the 80-foot high Carrick-a-Rede Rope

Bridge. (Absolutely optional to cross, don't push yourself to do it.) Afterwards your tour will return to central Dublin.

Giant's Causeway Day Trip from Dublin including Belfast

Tour's Highlights:

•Day Trip from Dublin to Giant's Causeway in Northern Ireland.

•Visit "King's Road" from Game of Thrones, aka Dark Hedges.

•Coastal beauty of the Giant's Coastal area.

•Attempt to cross the Carrick-a-Rede Rope Bridge. If you dare!

•On the return trip, gaze upon and visit Belfast.

•Air-conditioned transport.

Inclusions:

•Entrance fees to cross the Carrick-a-Rede Rope Bridge.

•Air-conditioned transport.

•Driver/guide.

Exclusions:

•Food and drink.

Additional:

•Infants are welcome, with their own parent provided car seat.

General Schedule:

•You will depart from central Dublin early in the morning in your luxury transport, headed towards Giant's Causeway.

•Next your journey brings you to Dark Hedges – King's Road for those Game of Thrones fans – where you will walk around, take some photos, and relax.

•Giant's Causeway is a beautiful rock formation created by a volcanic eruption. Truly a picturesque place to be, take lots and lots of photos while you're there!

•A brief stop in Belfast for the culture and history there before returning to central Dublin where the tour ends.

9Titanic Belfast Visitor Experience and Giant's Causeway Day Trip from Dublin – $81.58

Tour's Highlight:

•Full-day trip to the Titanic Visitor Experience and Giant's Causeway in Northern Ireland, same trip.

•Follow in the footsteps of the Titanic's voyage while you explore interactive galleries at the Titanic Visitor Experience.

•Visit the ocean exploration centre. Where you'll learn about the ins and outs of tracking the ocean's behavior.

•Travel along Antrim coastal Drive by luxury coach.

•Spend time relaxing at Giant's Causeway.

•Travel along the heart-pounding Carrick-a-Rede Rope Bridge, if you dare!

•Giant's Causeway & Visitor Heritage Centre for a two hour stop, the only tour in Dublin to offer you both attractions in one trip. An optional walking tour of Gant's Causeway Coast.

•Two-hour Titanic Experience "Explore the Shipyard, walk the decks, travel to the depths of the ocean and uncover the true legend of the Titanic in the city where it all began!".

•Premium tickets to walk across the Carrick-a-Rede Rope Bridge, an hour and thirty-minute stop, optional to cross.

Inclusions:

•Entrance fees.

•Professional guide.

•Transport by luxury, air-conditioned coach with free Wi-Fi.

•Entry to old Carrick-a-Rede Rope Bridge.

•Entry to Giant's Causeway Coastal Site.

•Entry to Titanic Belfast Visitor Experience.

Exclusions:

•Food and drink.

Additional:

•Wear good walking shoes and plan for all types of weather.

•Not wheelchair accessible.

•Make sure to check the pickup locations in the special requirements field when purchasing tickets.

General Schedule:

•Early in the morning you will depart from whichever specified hotel you chose in the luxury coach, listening to your guide introduce you to northern Ireland's history.

•Arrive at the Titanic Visitor Experience. The exhibition was opened on the one-hundred-year anniversary of the ship's tragic sinking.

•Enjoy a twenty-minute snacks/coffee break with a restroom break. If you would like to buy something for lunch from here you can do so.

•Enjoy the galleries as they speak of the tragic tale. Learn of the ship's construction, take part in the interactive displays and visit the Ocean Exploration Centre and discover state-of-the-art technology used to track ocean life.

•Lunch time. At the café before traveling to the rugged parts of Northern coast to see the Giant's Causeway Follow the scenic Antrim coastal Drive route, admiring the beauty as you journey to Dunluce Castle.

•After admiring Dunluce Castle, you will make your way toward Giant's Causeway to enjoy some relaxation while exploring and snapping beautiful photos.

•If you are brave enough, take a stroll across the Carrick-a-Rede Rope Bridge. If not, take some more lovely pictures of the scenery while others do.

•On the trip back to Dublin, enjoy a quick stop in the town Castlebelingham. Then journey back to central Dublin for the end of your tour.

Limerick, Cliffs of Moher, Burren and Galway Bay Rail Tour from Dublin

Tour's Highlights:

•Full-day trip by train and coach from Dublin to Limerick, Cliffs of Moher, the Burren and Galway Bay.

•A guided tour of Limerick where you'll learn about the city.

•See Bumratty Castle and Folk Village.

•Discover the Cliffs of Moher on the Wild Atlantic coast.

•Explore the Burren's lunar landscape and take photos.

•Scenic drive along the shore of Galway Bay.

Inclusions:

- Host on trains.

- Information pack.

- Reserved seats on train.

- Admission to Bunratty castle and Folk village.

- All travel by rail and coach from Dublin Heuston Station.

Exclusions:

- Gratuities. (Optional, but appreciated)

- Hotel pickup and drop-off.

- Food and drink.

Additional:

- There is a fee for infants four years old and younger, daily that is payable direct.

- Frequent stops for photos, shopping, bathroom, etc.

- Due to technical difficulties, it isn't uncommon for the itinerary to change.

- Wheelchair accessible, however the

passenger must have some mobility for buses/coaches.

•Mobility scooters cannot be accommodated.

General Schedule:

•Departure from Heuston station early in the morning on the train to Limerick; enjoy a breakfast if you choose to purchase one.

•Enjoy a tour of the city of Limerick; once the key settlement for Vikings in Ireland. More popularly known now as the setting of Frank McCourt's harrowing memoir Angela's Ashes.

•You will board the coach to Bunratty Castle and Folk Park, where you will explore the Castle and then enjoy a tour of Folk Park. You will get a general idea of Irish Village life in the turn of the 20th – century.

•Take a break for lunch at a traditional Irish pub; Gus O'Connor's Pub in Doolin.

After delicious food, and possibly a pint, travel to the Cliffs of Moher.

•After you have witnessed the beautiful Cliffs of Moher, enjoy a drive along the rocky coastal edge of the Burren and Galway Bay. You will eventually arrive in Galway, where depending on your arrival time; you may be able to enjoy a nice walk around before heading back to Dublin.

Shopping in Dublin

Dundrum Town Centre.

●Prime suburban shopping centre in Ireland. Many shops and restaurants to keep you occupied all day.

●House of Fraser and Havey Nichols are high end department stores. The mill Theater is also nearby, and a mini-golf park plaza cinema.

Henry Street.

●The main north-of-the-liffey shopping place. A street full of shopping malls, high street stores, Arnott's, and Dublin's oldest and largest department store.

●Stalls selling hats and handbags, sometimes you can buy cherries from a woman pushing a cart.

●Behind Arnott's you will find yummy foreign food to sample at the Epicurean Food Hall.

Moore Street.

- Dublin landmark famous for open air fruit and veggies market. Dublin's oldest.

- Open Monday through Saturday. Dozens of stalls selling produce at competitive prices. Also features ethnic shops behind the main market.

Clery's.

- A department store on O'Connell Street, dating all the way back to the 19th – century. The two-faced clock hanging outside its doors acts as a rendezvous point in the city.

- Affordable glamorous evening and casual clothes. Plus, a nail bar for manicures with the girls.

Temple Bar Markets.

- Three different markets for something different at each. On Saturdays visit the Temple Bar food market. Find it in the Meeting House Square.

- At Cow's Lane you'll find handmade

Irish crafts and designs at 20 different stalls. On Saturdays and Sundays in Temple Bar Square enjoy Vintage books and vinyl from Temple Bar Books Market.

The Harlequin.

●Mother/daughter vintage and repo boutique. Anything from casual wear to fancy evening wear under one roof.

George's Street Arcade.

●Affordable vintage and boutique mix, food markets, and collectible stalls. As well as little Cafes and a record shop.

●Described as random, diverse and cool. Built in 1881 as a Victorian shopping centre, remodeled but kept the unique atmosphere.

Powerscourt Townhouse Centre.

●High-end boutique shopping centre located inside of the Powerscourt family's old Georgian townhouse. Offers a wide range of upscale retail and design outlets.

●Shop for fashion, jewelry and antique vendors before having lunch/coffee at on of the cafes. Maybe treat yourself to a haircut/manicure at a salon.

Brown Thomas.

●Luxury shopping known as the Irish version of Selfridges. An upmarket combo of prêt-à-porter and haute couture clothing, accessories and makeup.

●On the opposite side of Grafton Street, the sister store – BT2 – caters to the younger generation. Hungry? Eat at "The Restaurant" where celeb chefs Domini and Peaches Kempt cook delicious food.

Grafton Street.

•The absolute must visit shopping area with shops ranging from quirky antique to upscale chic.

•Visit the St. Stephen's Green shopping

centre, a mix of shops and outdoor shopping galore. Plus, the eye-catching street performers.

•Take a photo with Molly Malone's stature, often accompanied by a leprechaun.

How to Save Money in Dublin

When planning a great vacay most people set their sights on fun, sun, great food and booze and entertainment. But it is also very important that you keep your wallet from over extending by forgetting that discounts are helpful! So, let's take a look at some great ways to save yourself some cash for a stress-free fun!

Start by traveling in the down time of the year when ticket prices are cheaper. April, may, or September for example. Try searching all year round for cheap/discounted tickets this can save up to three hundred dollars or more.

As fun as hotels are, they can be super expensive. So, looking at cheaper, less lavish options can really save you some fun cash! Check out sites like Airbnb for apartments, houses, bed and breakfasts, hostels, anything and everything. This can also save you up to three hundred dollars or more!

Rarely anyone ever thinks about vacationing and walking everywhere. But, it is something to be considered if you would like to save some spending money for the rest of Ireland. Taxis are tempting, but can rack up prices fairly quickly. Buses are relatively cheap, especially with a leap card – which offers discounted travel – but it can also rack up prices. The only mode of transportation that can truly save you the most money, is your own two feet!

However, if you are dead-set against walking and you choose to rent a car, it is highly suggested that you rent a small, compact one due to Dublin's roads being compact and narrow. Some of the streets are also marked for pedestrian only, which brings us back to the point of walking most places.

A super cool option is the Heritage Card. This offers you free entry to a vast majority of places around Dublin. It also lasts for a whole year, so don't worry about re-purchasing this during your stay. If you ever decided to come back during the year you have the card it is also still active. So, if you are planning to be a returning visitor it really is a smart choice for you!

There are also sites that offer discounted hotel rooms, up to 70% off, the unsold hotel rooms that need to be sold but are completely up to par. It is really smart to take advantage of this deal!

Most places you stay will offer you a complimentary breakfast, lunch or dinner depending on their policies. Take the opportunity. Food is pricey anywhere you go, especially if you are feeding multiple people. You can also find early bird specials at most places, sure you have to eat dinner a little earlier, but you get a discount and you can take leftovers back with you for later!

Groupons. Coupons. Discounts. Take advantage of any money you can save when planning your vacation. Especially during booking, plane tickets, hotels, anything that offers you a discount. Provided the discount is worth it, because the more money you save, the more you have for fun in Ireland! Seniors, students, and children may be up for special discounts. Make sure to ask wherever you buy a ticket.

Dublin's Nightlife

Top 10 Nightclubs

1 The Twisted Pepper.

●Books the hottest acts in the electric music scene also supports Dublin's music scene by setting up events to show some diverse tastes. The venue is over three floors that fills several different stages with different acts every Friday and Saturday.

2 The Workman's Club.

●Overlooking the Liffey, this club offers to both music and sometimes stand up comedy. Tons of space to dance with three floors and a rooftop garden. Top notch and affordable drinks.

3 The Grand Social.

●Live music, heavy drinking, and an impressive size. Voted Dublin's Best Live Music Venue. An amazing vibe with psychedelic marquee feelings. Take care of yourself with a quick bite to eat at the Beer Garden before a night of dancing and drinking.

4 The Academy, Middle Abbey Street.

●Tons of space for dancing and performers. Weekends are dedicated to alternative music. An electric dance atmosphere for the best clubbing night of your life.

5 The Button Factory.

●Right in the middle of Dublin's tourist and cultural hub. A fairly mixed group of people from students to regular clubbers to tourists and music lovers! The music scene is diverse enough with Indie, Techno DJ and Irish Folk.

6 The Village.

●Both a nightclub and a live music venue. Diverse music and a packed dance floor every night. Very popular among locals and tourists alike.

7 Lost Society.

●An 18th – century town mansion gone nightclub and bar. Vintage décor and a "vintage-indie" vibe. Basement DJ!

8 Pygmalion.

●Basement club under the Powerscourt Townhouse Centre. Truly Unique décor with exposed stone walls, a vintage photo booth and lots of nooks and crannies for possible romance? Anything is possible here! Young up-and-coming Irish acts and international DJS preform here.

9 Kyrstle.

●The socialite scene with athletes, models, celebs, its the place to be! A great mixture of music! Great night to be had here with your pals, or even solo because you never know when you'll meet someone interesting here.

10 Copper Face Jack's.

●A place for all! Young and old, local and

tourist. Find a great night here with friends, meet new and friendly people, maybe find a flirty night with an Irish cutie. Friendly atmosphere and great drinks!

The Best Free Events in Dublin

Dublin has a rich cultural atmosphere with plenty to do for free, from parks to galleries and libraries to browse. It also has a fairly large number of free events for tourists and locals alike to enjoy. Of course, some of these events have the option to pay for things like food and drink, but for the most part it is a free event for your viewing pleasure.

Below there are a few examples of the free events Dublin offers.

Temple Bar Night Market

Where: Temple Bar Square, Dublin.

When: Every Wednesday at 3pm to 8pm.

How much: Free.

An excellent showcase for local arts & crafts. Including, but not limited to, candles and jewelry made by the locals and sold for a fairly decent price.

Opera in the Open

Where: Civic Amphitheater, Wood Quay.

When: August 4th to August 25th from 1pm to 2pm.

How much: Free.

Opera in the Park at Dublin City Civil offices

With Operas such as The Gondoliers by Gilbert & Sullivan, 4th August. Acts & Galatea by Handel, 11th August. Die Fledermaus by J. Strauss, 18th August. Eugene Onegin by Tchaikovsky Musical, 25th August.

Dublin Rock n' Roll Festival

Where: Dame District & Camden Quarter, Dublin.

When: 5th to the 7th August.

How much: Free.

Come celebrate Rock n' Roll music with 50's cars and massive hairstyles! An event that is back by popular demand! If you are a rock fan, you will definitely have a great time!

Where: River Liffey.

When: 6th August.

How much: Free.

A tradition that dates back one-hundred years! Brave Irishmen and Women swim around the river Liffey while people cheer them on from the Quays, the boardwalks and Bridges! If you love to watch people swim, this is the event for you!

Where: Dublin Castle, Dame Street.

When: 6th August at 3pm to 5pm.

How much: Free.

Shakespeare is a literary god, known for many plays such as Hamlet, A Midnight's Summer Dream, Macbeth, and many other plays. However, there is a lesser known masterpiece that is very well-known to the people of Ireland. It addresses the social, political, economical and sexual forces behind the Irish Revolution. This play gives you a look at the year 1916 and Shakespeare's genius. A combination that makes for an amazing afternoon!

Ukulele Hooley

Where: Dun Laoghaire.

When: The 20th to the 21st of August.

How much: Free.

A fantastic Ukulele-packed weekend! With Ukulele masters and beginners' workshops, the Ukulele Bus Busk tour and Ukulele Hooley Open Mic night! The weekend will end with an eight-hour live concert by some of the most renowned Ukulele artists! A great way to spend a musical weekend!

Free Festivals by Month

Below you will find a list of free festivals for each month of the year, with brief descriptions of what to expect during your time there! A great event for each month with plenty to do!

<u>January.</u>

Temple Bar Tradfest.

A small, niche musical festival born in the year 2007 turned into a much larger, much more popular event in the past eleven years that it has been going on. The founders created this festival in hopes of providing the next generation of musicians with a place to showcase their talents by giving them a stage to blossom on. Plus, the opportunity to bring the fans of both Irish and international music together in happiness.

Over the years this festival has grown in size and in ambition from on of the smallest festivals in Ireland, to one of the largest musical festivals. Showcasing a large variety of music like Folk, nu-folk, and even Rock & Roll! Music-lovers will feel right at home here, and the energetic, electric atmosphere will pump you up even more as you enjoy every note of music!

Tradfest also offers the concert-goers a few historical places to view such as St. Patrick's Cathedral and the beautiful City Hall. You'll feel every note of the music and every single happy moment as you have a great time!

Some great reviews include:

"Temple Bar Tradfest is growing in strength every year." – Irish Independent.

"Temple Bar Tradfest has built its reputation as offering a chink of musical light in the dying days of January." – Irish Times.

February.

Jameson Dublin International Film Festival.

A festival committed to showing great Italian film as well as international film masterpieces. Italian cinema is known for providing its audience with diverse, dramatic and accomplished films – something the average film buff would find rave-worthy!

Directors such as Federico Fellini, Luchino Visconti, Pier Paolo Pasolini and many, many more have been featured here in the past. Each year the festival adds more classic directors and their masterpieces. People truly love it more each year!

This festival is fairly new, but with its vast success you wouldn't have guessed it. It is here that you will celebrate the best of Irish and world cinema with the possibility of meeting the screenwriters, directors and actors behind some of the most beautifully written films in the world.

St. Patrick's Day Parade & Festival.

Everyone in the world knows St. Patrick's Day as a great excuse to get plastered, and nobody does it quite like the Irish do! Not only is this a great holiday to get plastered, though, it is also a time of celebration for the Irishmen and women.

St. Patrick's Day (or St. Paddy's Day), is a great time of year for everyone, but imagine partying like the Irish do on this holiday. Can you imagine that?

Well you can make it a reality by joining in on the St. Patrick's Day Parade and Festival in Dublin! Here you will witness some truly amazing history celebration, get your drink on, and learn a little bit about what it means to be an Irishmen during the holiday!

The parade provides you with the celebration of St. Patrick, the man who banished the snakes so to speak, also known as The Feast of St. Patrick. You will see some of Europe's best performers and some killer pyrotechnics as well!

The festival is five days long, with exhibitions, street theater, amazing, booming fireworks and some truly fantastic company! The surrounding bars are always packed to the max during this time, from morning until night, so expect to wait a little bit if you choose to visit a pub or bar.

Dublin Bay Prawn Festival.

Where: Hawth Village

When: March 17th to March 19th

This festival will please anyone who loves to eat seafood, especially prawns! They are prepared every way imaginable – barbecued, whole, shelled, fried, skewered, marinated, sauced, however you may want it!

The Dublin Bay Prawn Festival

isn't just about the prawns, the menu is much larger than that with fish & chips, oysters, fish cakes, stir-fries, paella and smoked salmon are some examples of the delicious menu!

If you are impressed with the festival you can come back year-round for other fun activities and more delicious food! There are strolls, coastal adventures along the cliffs, enjoy the rich history and the best seafood any day of the year!

May.

Literary Festival.

The premier literary event for Ireland, this event gathers the finest writers in the world! Where they debate, provoke thought from your head, and delight the crowd with their beautiful, literary minds!

This event has been described as the country's "most successful and easily the best annual literary event" as well as "a stunning array of top international literary talent". You will not be displeased if you choose to attend this phenomenal event!

<u>June</u>

Dublin Writers Festival.

From all over the world fifty or so writers and poets will gather at this literary event for a truly magnificent banquet of readings, discussions and debates among some of the most talented writers!

Be sure not to miss out on the Rattlebag Poetry Slam, where the public compete for prizes!

Bloomsday Festival.

Held every year on the/ around the 16th of June, the day which Ulysses is set, and commemorating Bloom's "walk out". This festival is a week-long celebration with the readings from Joyce, performances, excursions and meals for a 1904 Dublin vibe the whole week!

July

World Performance Championship.

This festival lasts for three days in Dublin and two days in Cork, showcasing the best in international street performance, some interactive family activities, delicious artisan producers and street food from around the world to be enjoyed by many!

August

Ukulele Hooley.

Where: Dun Laoghaire.

When: The 20th to the 21st of August.

How much: Free.

A fantastic Ukulele-packed weekend! With Ukulele masters and beginners' workshops, the Ukulele Bus Busk tour and Ukulele Hooley Open Mic night! The weekend will end with an eight-hour live concert by some of the most renowned Ukulele artists! A great way to spend a musical weekend!

September

Culture Night Festival.

Venues and public spaces across Ireland host a free late-night entertainment across the country. This happens to celebrate arts, heritage and culture!

October

Dine in Dublin Festival.

Do you like to eat? Enjoy the different, rich and savory taste of Irish cuisine? Then this is the festival for you! A week-long food-based festival where well-known cafes and restaurants prepare a special menu for the duration, with a truly unique and delicious experience!

November

Dublin Book Festival.

One of Ireland's most successful book festivals, one that's been around since June 2006. This event shows, supports, and develops Irish Publishing by showing off and selling published books. Authors, editors and sponsors are also shown off to the public with respect. This event is a truly amazing and literary satisfying festival!

December

NYE Dublin Festival.

If you find yourself in Dublin during the new year you will not be disappointed. A new and exciting set of events will bring you into the new year with amazement and wonder, for two days and four amazing events from December 31st to January 1st.

Friends and family alike gather in the heart of Dublin as the Customer

House transforms into the center of the NYF Dublin countdown and New Year's Day celebration!

There are plenty of other events to enjoy in Dublin ranging from free to fairly expensive, these are just a few of the more popularly known free events and festivals.

Dublin's Museums and Art Galleries

Dublin has a massive art scene, seeing as it is not only the capital of the country, it is also the art capital of the country. People come to marvel at the beautiful museums and galleries within the city, art buffs from all over the world come to enjoy masterpieces by many famous artists such as Monet, Picasso, Mantegna, Titian and many other famous painters around history.

Not only is the country a beautiful, picturesque place to visit it is also a phenomenal place to paint, view art, and gather around the many art galleries in the City. Many of these art galleries are free to get into, and those that aren't do not carry a hefty price tag because it isn't about money – it's about enjoying the truly magnificent works of art that hang in the galleries around Dublin.

Below there is a list of the most

frequently visited museums and art galleries, and the known galleries to be free will also be marked as such to give you a leg up when planning your journey to Dublin.

This list is meant to help you express your love of art with like-minded people who just want to do the same!

1.)The Molesworth Gallery.

This gallery is small, but mighty sitting on Molesworth near the Leinstar House. Over two floors of an old Georgian townhouse, this gallery offers you the opportunity to view some of the most amazing contemporary art in the diverse art program. The gallery hosts eight single shows, and two group shows annually. Founded in 1999, this gallery supports up to 20 up-and-coming artists as well as a few well-known Irish artists.

The first floor features a revolving display of paintings, sculptures and prints. Critics lists frequently feature this art gallery on their 'Best contemporary

Art Galleries in Dublin' lists. You won't be disappointed if you choose to visit this art gallery.

2.)Dublin City Art Gallery; The Hugh Lane.

Rightfully named after the Irish Art collector Hugh Lane, this art gallery was first established in 1998. But, over one-hundred years before that Hugh Lane actually opened his own art gallery – The Municipal Gallery of Modern Art – on Harcourt Street. He did this as a temporary place to store all of his art, but unfortunately, he died in the sinking of the Lusitania in 1915.

This art gallery, Dublin City Art Gallery, has honored his memory and continued on his legacy in his absence. Located on Parnell Square in the Charlemont House, the gallery is a contrast to the Georgian landscape around it. Another art gallery that will blow your mind as you wander around with other guests enjoying the exhibits, and quite possibly a little history lesson about the man himself.

3.)Gallery of Photography Ireland.

Opened in 1978 by John Osman, this gallery is home to digital and film photography. The gallery was moved to its current location in 1995 with purposeful intentions, the gallery was specifically made for photography with dark rooms, and digital imagery facilities.

There are many free exhibits organized for the general public, showcasing the works of many Irish and global photographer's hard work and beautifully shot photos. The gallery also holds classes and workshops for those who would like to learn the craft themselves, so if you are going to be in Ireland for long enough and you are a photography buff you might want to consider taking one!

4.)Irish Museum of Modern Art.

In a mind-blowing clash between

contemporary culture and historical revenue, the Irish Museum of Modern Art is housed in a renovated 17th – century Hospital! The general vibe is that of Les Invalides in Paris, with formal facade and an elegant courtyard! In 1984 the hospital was restored and officially opened as the art gallery in May of 1991.

The gallery hosts a wide variety of revolving artists such as Irish designer Eileen Gray, as well as international artists like Philippe Perreno. Second Sight – a collection of 550 photographs created in the last 20 years by Dr. David Kronn – is one of the more recent exhibits. This art gallery is a fusion between old and new, and celebrates the past artistic achievements as well as the current by pushing cutting edge art for your enjoyment!

5.)Project Arts Centre.

This art gallery started as a one-day event, then blossomed into a three-week festival at the Gate Theater in 1966. Once its popularity exploded the event needed a place to call home, which prompted the purchase of two performance spaces inside of Temple Bar and a gallery.

Over the past four and a half decades, this art gallery has rapidly become the leading Art Gallery in contemporary artistic practices in Dublin and in Ireland. Not only have famous artists such as Gerard Byrne been featured here, but also musicians and actors like U2 and Liam Neeson have been featured here! This gallery has also hosted festivals such as the Dublin Writers Festival, Dublin Theater Festival and Dublin Fringe Festival.

6.)RUA RED.

Self-defined Art Centre of South Dublin, and home to all kinds of art aimed at a vast variety of audiences. Located in Tallaght, outside of Dublin City Centre, this art gallery/centre is focused on inspiring and encouraging Irish and international audiences. It collaborates with local festivals and organizations to bring you the most diverse and appealing line up of phenomenal works of art, programs and events!

It also holds other events such as theatrical productions, live music, film screenings, performance pieces and much more in its TWO galleries. Well worth the journey to Dublin City Centre.

7.)Rubicon Gallery.

Thought of in 1995 and brought to life on St. Stephen's Green, one of Dublin's famous landmarks, Rubicon Gallery is the main contributor of Ireland's Contemporary art scene. They strive to help Irish and international artists alike find their true potential and showcase it to the world! They are recognized in both Ireland and across the world as one of the best places to showcase rising talents.

Hosting around ten exhibitions annually, mostly solo shows but sometimes they will do group hosting. They also have a name abroad, hosting many art events, festivals and biennials. Rubicon also commissions new work, acting as a trampoline for new artists to jump right into the best of their potential.

8.)Temple Bar Galleries & Studios.

TBG+S for short, was established in 1983 by a group of artists and a few administrators, they became one of the first DIY Artist-centered events in Ireland. They rented an old unused factory and expanded over the years to host an entire block of Temple Bar. As Temple Bar became a tourist hot spot, the gallery began to contribute to and develop the area's revitalization in 1994.

Now, thirty or so years later, it continues to support local artists and international artists alike, as well as connecting the public with their amazing talent and work.

9.)The Douglas Hyde Gallery.

This gallery was founded in 1978 and officially became independent of Trinity College in 1984. In the following years this gallery was one of the only publicly funded artistic spaces in Ireland that was based on contemporary art. These days, The Douglas Hyde Gallery focuses on people who have been shunned based on being marginalized or simply overlooked both in Ireland and internationally.

It has two small, but functioning gallery spaces. The smaller gallery, which was added in 2001, hosts ethnographic and craft exhibits. It also hosts music events!

As mentioned above, there are a few completely free art galleries worth mentioning. A few have already been given descriptions so they won't be explained again.

Free Exhibits & Galleries

1.)Hugh Lane Gallery, Dublin.

This art gallery was already mentioned above, feel free to go back and read about this spectacular gallery!

2.)National Gallery of Ireland, Dublin.

Under the protection of the Oscar Wilde at the entrance of the National Art Gallery, this gallery overlooks Merrion Square. You will see some of the most beautiful religious paintings in Ireland. The painting "Marriage of Strongbow and Aoife" covers an entire wall in this art gallery. There is also a coffee shop within the gallery if you would like to catch a quick bite and a cappuccino.

3.)Science Gallery, Dublin.

This isn't technically an 'art' gallery. However, it is worth mentioning just based on the fact that it is interactive! You will understand how science works in real life, discussions and examples will be given and are encouraged to get involved in! You can keep an eye on which exhibits will be shown at which times on their website!

4.)Crawford Art Gallery, Dublin.

Located right beside the Opera house, this art gallery is renowned for its collection of Greek and Roman sculptures. They were brought to Cork in 1818 from the Vatican Museum in Rome. It is the regional art museum for Munster. The collection of over 2,500 works range from the 18th – century to contemporary Irish. It was formerly the Crawford School of Art and parts of the gallery date all the way back to 1724. In the year 2000 the new Modern exhibition wing was opened!

5.)Lewis Glucksman Art Gallery, Cork.

An award-winning gallery dedicated to art and architecture alike! Located off the University of Cork College (UCC) on the western road. It is incredibly easy to dwindle away an entire day wandering around this beautiful art gallery in Cork. Technically this art gallery is a learning institute that promotes research, creation and the exploration of visual art. It is different than the 'classic tourist trail' art galleries.

6.)Irish Museum of Modern Art, Dublin.

This was also already mentioned above, and is by far the most interesting (though that is opinion-based) with a backstory of restoration of an old Irish hospital!

There are many other exhibits and art galleries around Ireland and Dublin, these are just a few of the more mention-able ones. If I listed them all we would be here all day, don't be afraid to dive into researching many other art galleries around the Dublin area and Ireland entirely! Let your artist/art lover heart run wild!

Cool Facts About Dublin!

The natives speak a language called 'Dublinese' which is a cross between Dublin slang and curse words. Phrases such as "I'm on the lash", which means "I'm out drinking" are very a common thing. This alone is quite interesting and could provide you with some comedic encounters, plus a modern history lesson or two!

Have you ever wondered where the name Dublin came from? Well, it's pretty simple actually! The name Dublin (or Dubh Linn) comes from the old Gaelic phrase for "Black pool". It is also known to date back to Viking times, where they claimed Dublin as their settlement and named it "Norse Kingdom of Dublin". (As mentioned in the beginning of this guide.)

Just as with any place in the world, celebrities are known to step foot on Irish soil once in awhile, as well as some who are celebrated in the Dublin area. Which celebrities are celebrated here?

Those who are celebrated here include play write and Nobel-Prize laureate George Bernard Shaw, and writer/poet James Joyce. There are surely more celebrities who are well-known by the population of Dublin, these are just a few of the more notable.

Things __Not__ to Do in Dublin

Do not make the mistake off comparing Ireland to the British Isles. It is highly offensive as the country of Ireland has been independent for nearly one-hundred years. Only six of the counties of Ireland remain united within the UK, instead you should say 'Britain and Ireland' A native of Ireland will most likely strike up an argument or a fight with you if you insult their culture and their country, so steer clear of such offensive remarks.

Generally speaking, it isn't wise or respectful to discuss politics or religion while you are visiting Ireland, as it is a hot-button topic choice. However, if you find yourself further South and find a local that is willing to discuss it with you, have at it as long as you are respectful and sensitive about their troubled past!

Do not smoke indoors. Not in a restaurant, bar, nightclub, hotel, taxi, anywhere enclosed. Not only is it considered to be rude, it is also heavily enforced with the possibility of a hefty fine if you are caught. Absolutely do not smoke in a car with a child as this is 100% outlawed in Ireland!

This next point is more common sense than anything else. Do not butcher the Irish language. If you aren't sure how to say something in Irish (Gaelic) then do not attempt to do so. English is a language that is very commonly spoken in Ireland, and while it isn't their primary language per se, the natives use it more often. So, don't be afraid of offending someone with a language barrier that isn't there.

In Ireland, it is customary for someone to buy a round of drinks, and then when the round starts to dwindle the next person buys a round and so on and so forth. However, if you fail to do so, if it very offensive and may get you the stink eye from a lot of people! So be sure to share the wealth when the wealth is shared with you! Also, random tidbit of information, it is not customary to tip the person behind the bar, but I'm sure they would appreciate it!

Do not complain about the weather. They know it is rainy and sometimes unpredictable, and it makes for terrible small talk anyways.

Do NOT bring up leprechauns. Ever. Not to be funny or to be cute. A lot of Irishmen find it heavily offensive as the bearded fairy is also linked to hurtful Irish stereotypes from the past. It has nothing to do with Irish culture or their religion, it is more of a souvenir and gimmick seller. Natives don't find it to be all that 'charming'.

Don't shorten St. Patrick's Day to "St. Patty's Day". It is highly offensive as it is the national holiday in Ireland, and not just an excuse to get blackout drunk. However, if you do shorten it, make sure you use the correct diminutive form "St. Paddy's Day".

Do not misunderstand their uses of the word 'sorry'. Irishmen and women are quick to apologize when they bump into you, and sometimes the word is used instead of 'excuse me' and that will make it sound as if it is a question more than a statement. Do not get offended or misunderstand what they are trying to say.

Absolutely do not object to swearing. Irishmen and women are very likely to use casual swearing. It is just how they speak day-to-day! So, if you object to swearing you might want to think about vacationing somewhere else! A comedian explains that the Irish swear so much because of their adaption to the English language 'not suiting their souls'!

Don't stick to a bucket list of places you would like to visit! Native Irishmen love it when tourists attend the lesser known places such as Donegal's Slieve League Cliffs, the Beara Peninsula and the Carrick-a-Rede rope bride in County Antrim! So, if you'd like to earn some brownie points with the locals, perhaps you should look into the lesser known places!

With some of the best meat and dairy products in the world, it is highly advised that you don't limit yourself to eating primarily in pubs! Branch out and eat some of the amazing Irish cuisine that the restaurants and cafes have to offer you!

Driving in Ireland. Oh boy. It is an adventure of its own, and it is highly advised that you do NOT forget your manners when driving! The roads are very narrow, so it is customary for one person to pull over to allow another to safely pass them. It is also common for one to greet another with one index finger while driving, even if you do not know that person! Motorists are also known to flash their hazards and wave in the rear-view mirror to show appreciation for letting them past!

50 More Facts About Dublin

(A few you may not necessarily need to know)

1.) Dublin's O'Connell Bridge was once made of rope and could only support a man and his donkey. Wood replaced the rope in 1801 and then in 1863 the current concrete replaced it. It was once called 'Carlisle Bridge'.

2.) Another O'Connell Bridge fact is the bridge is wider than it is long, the only traffic bridge in Europe with these dimensions.

3.) Dublin has a second O'Connell Bridge across the pond in St. Stephen's Green.

4.) Though Dublin has a generous number of mountains, yet none of them meet the criteria to be considered 'mountains'. The tallest mountain, the Sugarloaf, is a mere 1,389 feet above sea level.

5.) RTE -- the headquarters of the national television broadcaster -- in

Montrose was originally built to be used as an abattoir.

6.) Dublin's oldest traffic lights, built in 1893, are standing by the Renault garage in Clontarf. They were installed outside of the first Irishmen to own a car, Fergus Mitchell's home.

7.) The Temple Bar received its name for two controversial reasons; it housed the first Jewish temple built in Ireland, and the word 'bar' refers to the Catholic's refusal to allow Jewish people to enter any adjoining commercial places.

8.) In the year 1761, a gypsy family from Navan was refused entry to Dublin. They settled in the outskirts and created the town of Rush, where two-hundred and fifty years later the population can trace their roots back to the family.

9.) Between the hours of 5:30pm on Friday evening and 3am the following Monday, Dubliners drink 9,800 pints an hour.

10.) Dublin is the most popular stag and hen party place, with an estimated six-hundred 'pre-wedding sessions' every weekend.

11.) Harold's Cross received its name because of a tribe -- the Harold's -- who lived in the Wicklow Mountains. The Archbishop of Dublin wouldn't let them enter the city.

12.) Leopardstown was once known as Leperstown.

13.) Dublin's average twenty-five year olds still live with their parents.

14.) Ireland isn't the only country with a 'Dublin'. The United States has twelve places and Australia has six.

15.) In the 1700s, an extremely wealthy gambler named Buck Whaley made an equivalent to seven million dollars a year. He lived in what is now the Catholic University of Ireland in St. Stephen's Green. Eventually, he went broke and left Ireland with gambling debts. He had a shipload of Irish soil imported so he could be buried in it.

16.) The statue of Queen Victoria in Sydney, Australia was a gift from Ireland in 1988 when the city had its 200th anniversary. It was once in the Garden of Leinstar house.

17.) In 1988 a cake of 190 pounds was made, and it stood untouched inside the Mansion House until 1991 when it was finally thrown out.

18.) Strangers are very likely to be given a drink from a local, more so than another local of Ireland entirely.

19.) Dublin City has forty-six rivers running through it. A few are the River Swan and the Poddle (once known as the 'Tiber' or the River Salach 'dirty river').

20.) Dublin has its own 'Romeo' named St. Valentine, the saint for lovers all over. his remains are lying inside of Dublin's Whitefrair Street Church, many visit him each year. The Vatican no longer recognizes him as a saint, though.

21.) The statue in Phoenix Park is commonly known as the 'Floozy in the

Jacuzzi'. The unique nicknames don't stop there! A statue at the bottom of Grafton Street is known as the 'tart with the cart'. The women at the Ha'penny Bridge are known as the 'Hags with the bags'. There are many more unique statue nicknames around!

22.) Montgomery Street was once home to over 1,600 prostitutes. It was once known as the 'Monto' locally and even had a song named after it called 'Take Me up to Monto'.

23.) In the eighteenth century, a man named Henry Moore, Earl of Drogheda was in charge of naming the streets. he named a handful after himself such as; Henry Street, Moore Street, Earl Street and Drogheda Street.

24.) In 1966, Nelson's Pillar was blown up to celebrate/ mark the fiftieth anniversary of the 1916 rising. It is now a dusty heap in a valley somewhere in County Wicklow.

25.) Leinstar House was built for the Duke of Leinstar, at the time the most fashionable part of Dublin was the

North side. And when he was asked why he planned to build on the South side he simply said 'Where I go, fashion follows me!' He was right. To this day, the South side of Dublin remains the fashionable place to be.

26.) Tallaght -- meaning The Plague Cemetery -- is one of the oldest place names.

27.) The Seven areas of Dublin that end in O are; Rialto, Marino, Portobello, Phibsboro, Monto, Casino and Pimlico. Very few -- 1 in 20,000 Dubliners -- can name them by heart.

28.) Kevin Street Garda Station once housed the Archbishop of Dublin.

29.) When the capitol was much smaller Trinity College was once named 'Trinity College Near Dublin'.

30.) A fountain in College Green -- depicting ghastly statues of angels -- stands where a statue of King Billy riding a horse used to be. That particular statue was blown up six times before it was completely wrecked by a bomb in 1946.

31.) Inside Temple Bar, the Oliver St. John Gogarty sells the most dearly held pint in Ireland. It costs €7.15.

32.) A pint of Guinness, depending on the part of Dublin you go to, can cost as little as €3.

33.) North Side Women are very likely to get pregnant from casual sex -- at least   33 women. Whereas women from Meath are the least likely to get pregnant from casual sex.

34.) An average Dubliner spends €81 a night and makes €34,800 per annum.

35.) Dublin produces ten million pints of Guinness per day.

36.) The Phoenix Park is the largest park in Europe.

37.) You can ride a bicycle from one side of Dublin to the other in half an hour.

38.) Dublin has more art galleries per capita than any other city in Europe.

39.) You can pick from over one thousand pubs in Dublin to drink in.

40.) Unlike the United States the drinking age in Dublin is eighteen years old.

41.) Dublin's population is over 1.66 million people.

42.) Due to St. Patrick banishing them, the country of Ireland has no 'snakes'.

43.) Bram Stoker was born in Clontarf, and the world-famous novel Dracula was said to have come from the Irish words "Droch ola" meaning bad blood.

44.) The band U2 was given the honorary title of 'The freedom of the Dublin City' which gives them the privilege to partake in free sheep grazing at St. Stephen's Green.

45.) The Oscar statuette used at the Academy Awards was designed by

Cedric Gibbons, who was born in 1823 in Dublin.

46.) The MGM lion, Clarence, was bred in the Dublin Zoo.

47.) Brazen Head is the oldest pub in Ireland, and a pub has stood there since 1198.

48.) The Dubh Linn used to be a lake that the Vikings used to trade ships and it connected to the River Liffey via the River Poddle.

49.) In the year 988 AD Vikings founded Dublin.

50.) There are fewer pubs per head in the city than in other European capitals.

Dublin is a really phenomenal place to visit any time of the year, for business or for pleasure. There is so much to do and so much to see, great food to eat, drinks are always enjoyed and the company is truly one of the best experiences in the world. You couldn't possibly pick a better vacation spot, with so much at your fingertips and many amazing excursions, hikes, tours and museums to occupy all of your time while you are here.

There is so much to do you may feel like you won't have enough time to do it all! But there is always next time, isn't there? Each returning visit offers you the opportunity to visit the things you missed, and maybe make an excursion to some of the lesser known villages, towns and cities in Ireland. You won't be bored during your stay in the gorgeous, lush country of Ireland!

Hopefully this little guide helped convince you to visit, and if you were already planning on visiting hopefully it helped you find cheaper prices, perfect dining, the best schedule for the duration of your stay, and maybe even a few little Dublin facts you may not have known before.

Don't forget to show off your wonderful trip with lots of photos, souvenirs, and maybe a gift or two for your friends and family who didn't accompany you on the journey. Definitely make it a priority to visit again if you didn't get enough of the rich culture, beautiful scenery, and amazing cuisine/alcoholic beverages while you were here!

Enjoy your stay in the magnificent and truly wondrous city of Dublin, Ireland!

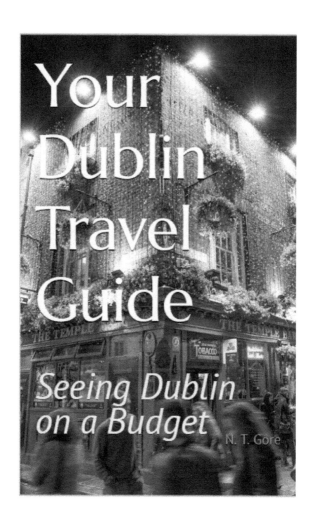

Your Dublin Travel Guide

Seeing Dublin on a Budget

N. T. Gore

CPSIA information can be obtained
at www.ICGtesting.com
Printed in the USA
LVHW031716140519
617804LV00013B/1183/P